Copyright © 2022 by Barrett Williams

All rights reserved. No part of this publication may be reproduced, stored or transmitted in any form or by any means, electronic, mechanical, photocopying, recording, scanning, or otherwise without written permission from the publisher. It is illegal to copy this book, post it to a website, or distribute it by any other means without permission.

First Edition

ISBN: 9798362340179

HOW TO MAKE MONEY FLIPPING MOTORCYCLES FOR PROFIT

*USING THE PROVEN **MONEYBIKE FORMULA** TO GENERATE PROFIT FROM BUYING AND SELLING MOTORCYCLES.*

BARRETT WILLIAMS

Contents

1. Introduction 4
2. Why Motorcycles? 7
3. Before You Start 10
4. The Moneybike Formula 17
5. Setting up Shop 64
6. Case Studies 80
7. Example Bill of Sale 89
8. Example Spreadsheets 90
9. References 97

1 Introduction

I think I was probably 38 years old the first time I saw a motorcycle, up close, and in person. At that point, I had been all over the world serving in the military, and for whatever reason, never had any real contact with motorcycles.

My buddy was showing me a new zero-turn mower he had just bought that was stored in his shed. While gawking at the cool new mower, I saw a yellow fender poking out of some debris over in the corner. I asked him, "what is THAT thing?!".

"Oh, that's the Angry Chui Wawa!" he said. "It's my 1998 Suzuki Savage 650. It's a motorcycle!"

He moved the junk from around it and I got my first good look at it—it was awesome!

There was something about the bike that just looked like the coolest thing I had ever seen. Maybe it was all the chrome (which was pretty rusty and dirty), or the design of the bike, who knows. I thought it was the most awesome looking thing I had ever seen.

As it turns out, he had this motorcycle sitting in his shed for years. Several years before I saw it, this motorcycle was his daily driver. He rode it back and forth to work every day, and in just about any weather. Then, he got cancer that almost killed him. After finally beating cancer, he got back on the bike one day and almost dropped it at a stoplight. He was still weak from his recovery, and the motorcycle was too heavy for him. He managed to ride it home, parked it in the shed, and never rode it again. For those of you that are familiar with bikes, Suzuki Savage 650 motorcycles are very small which tells you how weak he must have been to not be able to hold it up!

A couple weeks later I traded a Nintendo Wii and a Jackson Guitar for the bike. He trailered it from his shed to my garage and I was the proud owner of a 1998 Suzuki Savage LS650 that was covered in dirt dobber wasp nests, had rusted chrome, was covered in a patina of filth front to back, and wouldn't start.

That bike was a great learning experience for me. It prompted me to take a Motorcycle Safety Course and get a motorcycle cycle driver's license.

Eventually, I fixed all the mechanical problems with the bike and got it all cleaned and detailed. It was an awesome bike, and I learned many lessons about motorcycles from owning that Suzuki Savage. I ran out of gas on the bike (twice) and learned how reserve fuel works. My friend put a louder exhaust on the bike (which is why he called it the Angry Chui Wawa) and I learned all about how air/fuel mixtures work in a carburetor. I learned the relationship between the exhaust pipe and the carburetor. I learned how hard it is to mount new tires with tubes onto spoke rims and how it's so much easier to have a shop do that task for you. Finally, I learned that motorcycles are one of humanities best accomplishments in balancing form and function. Motorcycles are a piece of artwork that we get to ride.

Motorcycles are primarily works of art, and secondarily modes of transport. When flipping bikes, it's important to always keep that in mind. People don't buy motorcycles to get from point A to point B—that's what Honda Civics are for. People buy motorcycles because they look badass and are exhilarating to ride.

This book takes you through my proven process of flipping bikes for profit. I call it *The Moneybike Formula*. It's the process I've used, over and over, to profit from buying and selling motorcycles. In this book I describe the lessons I've learned flipping bikes that have culminated to this specific process. I've done this for a while now, and I've made thousands of extra dollars. My process works for me, and it can work for you too.

2 Why Motorcycles?

Think about what all successful business ventures have in common. First and foremost, they all meet some kind of customer need. So, they either solve a customer's problem or provide a customer a desired good or service. In the case of flipping bikes, we're solving a customer's problem and providing them a good or service. Their problem is that they are not cool enough. Buy a motorcycle—problem solved! Ok so maybe what we're doing here is solely providing a desired good, or product.

It's important to think about the motorcycles we're going to eventually sell as just that—products. A motorcycle is a great product to sell for a lot of reasons.

First, motorcycles are in demand. According to the U.S. Bureau of Transportation Statistics, motorcycle registrations have consistently topped 8 million per year, for the past 10 years.

In fact, in 2020 motorcycles were ridden over 17.6 billion miles in the United States.[1]

Looking forward into the future, according to Fortune Business Insights, the demand for motorcycles in expected to increase by 8.4%, each year, between 2022 and 2029.[2]

People are demanding motorcycles, and this trend will continue for the next several years.

When "flipping" anything, they key is to be able to buy low and sell high. That's common sense. With motorcycles, there are plenty of motorcycles available in the marketplace that are prices very low, with tons of potential. There are many reasons for this. Typically, it's because the owner has "fallen out of love" with the motorcycle and see it simply as taking up space. He or she is willing to take a reduced price to free up the space and get it out of his barn, or shed, or yard. On the flip side, once the bike has been properly refurbished (which you will learn how to do in this book), it once again reveals it's badassery and will fetch a premium to a new owner.

Again, I'll say it—motorcycles are art that we can ride. As such, their old owners "divorce" themselves from the bikes and the new owners "fall in love" with the bikes. Buying a motorcycle is very much an emotional event. It is for me, you and everyone else who buys a bike. However, when selling a bike, there's very little emotion. It's in the way, taking up space in the seller's garage or sitting in their yard, and they are ready to liquidate it for cash.

All of that allows us to buy low, sell high in a way that we just can't do with Honda Civic cars or John Deere riding mowers. Motorcycles are less of a commodity and more like buying and selling art (I'm guessing here, I've never bought and sold art). That means that our job, as the motorcycle flippers, is to get the princess ready for the dance. We take the ugly duckling (that probably doesn't even function) and we clean it, fix it, polish it, and resell it. We're adding value to the process and at the end of the day, everyone wins. The old owner gets a hunk of junk out of their shed, the new owner gets a dazzling beauty of a motorcycle to enjoy, the motorcycle gets to see the light of day again, and we make a tidy profit for our good deed of rescuing one more bike.

3 Before You Start

There are a few things to think about before you get started. What you don't want to do is get neck deep into this effort only to realize that you are breaking some state law, or you don't have the time to devote, or there is some other issue. You run the risk of ending up with a broken-down motorcycle in *your* garage that, for some reason, you can't fix up and resell. Then, you become one of the many sellers looking to liquidate your motorcycle for cash. If that happens to you, by the way, give me a call and I'll make you an offer!

But seriously, here are a few things you want to consider before setting up shop.

3.1 State Laws and Regulations

I'm in Texas. In my state, I'm allowed to buy and sell four (4) vehicles before I'm required to get a dealer's license. In Texas, getting a dealer's license means I need a physical location, of a certain size, staffed regularly, so on, and so forth. So, if this just a side hustle for me, and I have a full-time job, then I need to be aware of this limitation. Four bikes per year, that's it. However, my wife can also sell four bikes per year as well.

Be sure to research these vehicle dealer laws in your state. Here is a good Google Search phrase that you can use (replace "Texas" with your own state):

> "How many vehicles can I sell in a year without a dealers license in Texas?"

Copy and paste that phrase into your Google search bar. Google is great and will point you in the right direction. What you will find is that some states have a number limit like Texas. Some states, like Oklahoma, allow you to sell as many as you'd like so long as you are not doing it for profit (oh no!).

Be sure to have a good understanding of how to operate within the law. You should be able to decipher the law enough to know what you can and cannot do within the bounds of the law. If necessary (usually not), get an hours' worth of time from a lawyer to help you understand the law. If you need a dealer's license, then be sure to research what all that means. Costs associated with getting a dealer's license typically include:

- Cost of the license itself
- Cost of dealer plates

- Cost for surety bonds (this is insurance the state makes you have in order to protect consumers from malpractice and fraud)

If you're in Texas, things get more complicated with a license. You'll need to research the other requirements such as:

- Do you need a car lot (er, motorcycle lot)?
- Do you need a building?
- Do you need to have the lot staffed for a minimum number of hours each week?
- Do you need phone, internet, etc?

In many states, you can flip a certain number of bikes before you get to the point that you need to think about getting a dealer's license. Be sure to understand what that number is.

Again, for me and my wife the law allows us plenty of bikes we can flip, per year, for extra income, without needing a dealer's license.

3.2 Time

This formula for successfully flipping motorcycles will take some of your time. You're not going to farm everything out for other people to do. You're going to do a lot (or all) of the work yourself. You will be researching good deals to buy. You will be driving to pick up your motorcycle. You will be spending time researching and fixing the bike's issues. You will be spending time detailing the bike. And finally, you will be meeting with potential buyers to sell your motorcycle. All of that takes time.

What I have found is that the formula I've outlined in this book takes about 20 hours of labor to flip a bike. That is an estimate. Some bikes a little more, some a little less. But 20 hours is a good estimate. What exactly does that mean? Well, it usually goes something like this:

- 6 hours to find the bike
- 10 hours to refurbish the bike
- 4 hours to sell the bike

These are man-hours. What that means is that the six hours to find the bike may be in 20-minute chunks spread out over two weeks as you browse Facebook Marketplace. The 10 hours to refurb the bike will be divided up into an hour here, two hours there, four hours on that Saturday, etc. Think of it like clocking into work. If you had a timecard, and tracked your time, those numbers would be what all your minutes would tally up to but spread over a few weeks.

If you don't have a minute of free time, this whole endeavor probably won't work out too well for you. So, think about how much free time you typically have. Do you have enough time to flip motorcycles? Yes? Great! Let's move on.

3.3 Skills and Knowledge

When I started flipping motorcycles, I had never even touched one. I had zero experience doing any kind of maintenance on a motorcycle whatsoever. None.

Here's what I quickly learned. In terms of vehicles and their complexity, motorcycles are on par with riding lawn mowers.

"What?! Are you saying my awesome Suzuki Boulevard C50 is no more complicated than my John Deer LA154 riding mower?!"

Yes. That's exactly what I'm saying. Motorcycles are way cooler looking than riding mowers, no question there! But as far as complexity, they are about the same.

If you've ever done any kind of maintenance on a riding mower then you are ahead of the curve. If you've ever done maintenance on a car or truck, then you are lightyears ahead of the curve.

The skill involved in motorcycle maintenance involves physical dexterity, and a few techniques. But not as much skill as working on a car or truck. Motorcycles are lighter and their components are much easier to access then their four wheeled cousins. You just don't need as much technique under your belt to successfully maintain a motorcycle. There's less going on, design wise, than a car or truck. For example, take a look at the suspension on your car's front, driver-side wheel. Hole smokes! Complicated! There is all kinds of stuff going on there! Now look at a motorcycle's front wheel—forks. Simple. It's like calculus versus simple addition.

If you've maintained a riding mower, you can maintain a motorcycle.

The great thing about today's world is that you can start an endeavor with zero knowledge. That's because the knowledge you will need is on the internet or, for flipping bikes, in a readily available maintenance manual. The knowledge is out there, and you can get it as you need it. You don't have to have it all up front at once.

3.4 Space

Before you start you will need to ensure you have a little space to work. Honestly, you don't need much.

Motorcycles just aren't that big. But you do need enough space so that the bike can sit out of the way, covered and secured, until it is finished and sold.

In addition to space needed for the actual bike, you need space for other stuff to. You need some free space for parts to sit, protected, until they are reassembled on the bike. It's not uncommon to need a place for a removed gas tank for a week or so. Having some empty shelving, or similar storage space, is a good idea.

You'll also need space for your tools—wrenches, socket sets, screw drivers, etc. When I started, I had one of those rolls around toolboxes. The top of the toolbox was a work surface with a rubber mat and the box itself had 6 drawers. It was perfect to get me started. I also had an area in my garage that I could park the bike where it was out of the way and covered.

Today, I have used some of my profits to buy pegboard, more shelving, and some lighting. I still only have room for 1 bike at a time. But, for me purposes, that's plenty of room.

4 The Moneybike Formula

Every business uses a formula. Another term for the formula is the business model. Basically, it's details of how a business takes inputs, adds value, and produces outputs for profit.

For example, think about a bakery. To be successful, the bakery needs capital (stuff and money), labor (workers and their time), and a business model. The capital part is pretty self-explanatory—a retail location, some cash in the bank, ovens to bake the bread, bags of flour, sugar, etc., etc. The labor is self-explanatory—workers, supervisors, a manager, etc.

But the model part, the formula, is the part that really sets the bakery apart from the other bakeries in town. The formula includes all the processes, procedures and techniques a business uses. Like any formula, it's made up of components, or pieces. Put all the pieces together and you have the formula.

Maybe the bakery has business hours from 6am to 2pm. Maybe it's a 24-hour bakery—a pretty different business model. The hours it chooses is a component of the overall formula. The wholesale supplier it uses to purchase the flour—part of the formula. The recipes it uses—part of the formula. Do they deliver? Cater?

Wedding cakes? Donuts? Kosher products? Do they advertise on TV? Radio? Internet? All elements of their formula that makes them different and (hopefully) successful.

This book describes the Moneybike Formula. The Moneybike Formula is proven in that I've used it many times and it has always worked. I've always profited using this formula. Can you change up the elements in this formula and be successful? Maybe, and you're welcome to try. But for the purposes of this book, I'm going to stick to the formula and show you what I know works. Sometimes I try new things with the formula. That, by the way, is called innovation—trying to stuff to see if you can get a better result. Again, you are encouraged to tinker with the formula. But when you do, understand that your change may cause you to be less successful. That the experimenting part. Sometimes it works out and sometimes it doesn't.

I'm going to give you the formula in outline form, then I'm going to expand on each element.

Here's the formula:

- Sourcing Filter: Potential Moneybikes found on Facebook Marketplace or Craigslist
    - Manufacturer: Honda, Suzuki, Kawasaki, or Yamaha
    - Price: $2000 or less
    - Year: 2000 or newer
    - Profit: $1500 or more, 50% ROI or more
- Acceptable Problems
    - Neglected Nelly – parked for long term, carbs or injectors gunked with old fuel
    - Broken Betty - A single maintenance issue (external to engine)
    - Dropsy Daisy – the bike was tipped over why at a standstill. Gas tank and other components may be slightly damaged
- Unacceptable Problems
    - Sideswipe Sally - bike dropped during a moving vehicle accident and entire side is scraped up
- Refurbish Bikes to the following standards:
    - Maintenance issues corrected
    - New oil, new oil filter
    - Cleaned air filter (or new if it was in bad shape)
    - New spark plugs
    - Gear oil inspected, replaced if necessary
    - Brake pads inspected, replaced if necessary
    - Battery tests good and within 3 years of manufacture date
    - Tires good and within 5 years of manufacturer date
    - Fork seals have no leaks
    - Missing or non-OEM parts replaced with OEM parts
    - Bike detailed front to back
    - Corrosion removed
    - Painted surfaces cleaned and waxed
    - All chrome polished
    - Rubber/black plastic restored
    - All lighting works
    - Horn works
    - Odometer functions work
    - 2 sets of keys with nice keychains
    - Clear title in your name, in hand
    - 1 or 2 enhancements (brand new things) added.
- Finished product listed on Facebook and CycleTrader

So that's it. That's the formula. Using that formula, you'll need to provide the following inputs (capital and labor):

- Capital - $1,500 - $3,000 in starting cash to buy the bike and the stuff you'll need to refurbish it
- 20 hours (or so) of labor

If you input those two things into the formula above, you'll end up with roughly $1,500 in profit with a return on your investment of 50% in about a month. If you do some quick math, you'll notice that you're making about $75/hour ($1,500 in profit for 20 hours of work). Not too shabby. Plus, you get to play with cool motorcycles. Can't beat it!

Let's take a real close look at that model and understand each item in detail.

4.1 Sourcing Filter

A "sourcing filter" is a method of looking at everything for sale and filtering out the stuff we don't want. A shopping list is a sourcing filter. When we look for a bike to flip, we use our sourcing filter to help us pick out a bike that has a good potential of being a Moneybike. We'll need to accomplish more detective work to be sure, but the sourcing filter gives us good potential bikes to start with.

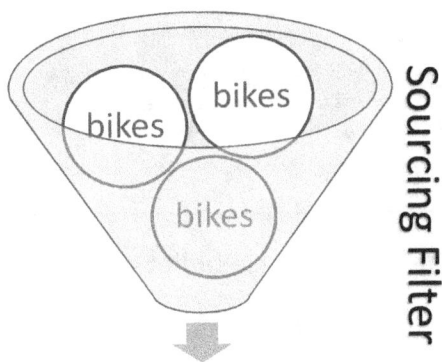

Potential Moneybike

Basically, we're looking for a bike that meets a specific set of standards (defined in our Sourcing Filter) that is being offered at a wholesale price. Wholesale means much less than what we would find the bike valued for on Kelly Blue Book, for example.

There are several reasons sellers offer their bikes at wholesale prices. Many times, it has to do with the condition of the bike—they need work. That's what we're looking for.

The box below is the sourcing filter that we will use to find our candidate Moneybikes.

- Source: Facebook and Craigslist
- Manufacturer: Honda, Suzuki, Kawasaki, or Yamaha
- Price: $2000 or less (i.e., wholesale price)
- Year: 2000 or newer
- Profit: $1500 or more, 50% ROI or more

Let's look at each of these bullet points in detail.

Source

Facebook Marketplace is probably the best source to find potential Moneybikes. Additionally, Facebook has Buy and Sell groups that are local to your area. If you're on Facebook, then chances are you are also members of some of your local Buy and Sell groups. However, I've been much more successful looking through the Marketplace rather than the groups.

Craigslist is another potential source. Like Facebook, you can select bikes within some radius of where you live, and filter on other things like price, make and model.

Make (i.e., Manufacturer)

The next part of our sourcing filter is the manufacture—Honda, Suzuki, Kawasaki, or Yamaha. We stick to these four manufactures for three reasons.

First, these bikes are called "metric" bikes. The reason for this is because they are assembled using metric sized components and require metric size tools. If you are a novice mechanic, using metric sizes is easier to understand than standard sizes that use fractions. This isn't a huge deal really, but it just seems easier for a newbie to understand that a 12mm wrench is smaller than a 14mm wrench. Most importantly though, we are not looking for bikes that are *either* metric or *standard*. In other words, we need to pick *only* metric bikes (the manufacturers listed) or *only* standard bikes (Harley-Davidson). Why do we want to only exist in one of these two worlds—metric or standard? One answer is cost. If we want to keep the amount of money we need to invest as small as possible, then we need to pick metric or standard bikes so that we only need to invest in a set of metric or standard tools. If we pick metric, we have 4 manufacturers to choose from (Honda, Suzuki, Kawasaki and Yamaha). The designs of these bikes are all very similar. If we choose standard, then we only really have one manufacturer to choose from— Harley Davidson. You'll learn why we've picked metric over standard in the next couple of paragraphs.

Another reason we chose these manufacturers (and the metric side of the motorcycle world) is because of price. We're looking for bread-and-butter bikes, that are plentiful in the marketplace, that can be resold at a price point which appeals to the widest audience. If I'm flipping houses, I'm flipping $200k houses, not $2 million dollar houses. The reason is because there are more folks looking to buy a house for $200k than $2M. Same with bikes. There are more buyers for a $4,500 bike then a $12,000 bike. So, we stick to bread-and-butter bikes that are plentiful to find and whose buyers are plentiful as well. The market for $4,500 bikes is way more thriving than the market for $15,000 bikes.

Lastly, these bikes hold their value over time. Take a look at this figure:[3]

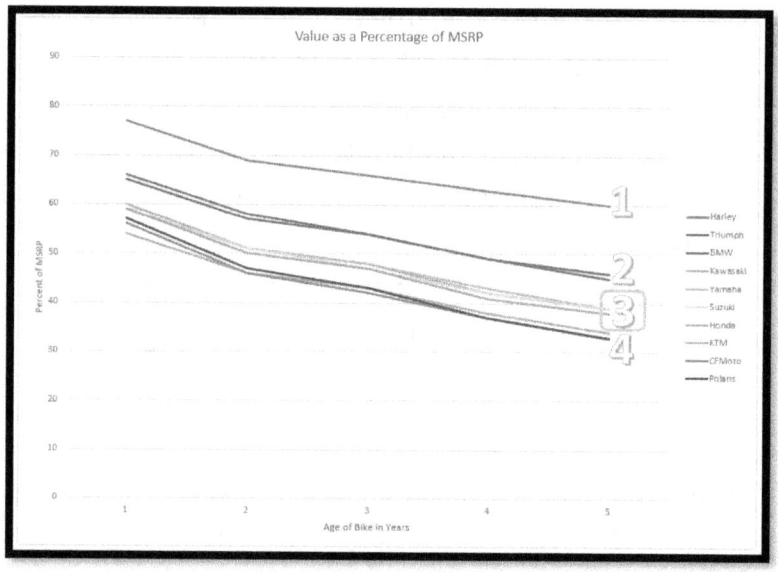

This chart shows the value as a percentage of MSRP (the original price), over the course of 5 years. As we move to the right side of the chart, we see that the value of each type of bike decreases versus its original price. However, we see that some bikes decrease in value faster than others. In fact, there seems to be groups of manufacturers that decrease similar amounts. That's the "1, 2, 3, 4" numbers. That shows the grouping. The manufacturers in our formula are in group 3 indicated by the outline.

We avoid Harley-Davidson bikes because they are too expensive. We avoid BMW and Triumph bikes because of cost as well, but also because of complexity of maintenance. I won't get into that here, but these bikes are more complex than group 3 bikes.

We avoid group 4 bikes because they lose value too fast. Group 3 bikes are in the goldilocks zone—just right! They are plentiful in the marketplace, they are priced to appeal to a wide audience, they are all maintained with metric tools, and they are relatively easy to work on—goldilocks.

Price

For these metric bikes, what you will typically find is that a seller who is "divorcing" themselves from a bike will part with it for about $2,000 or less. That's what we're after. The reason is because we're going to spend about $1,000 on it and resell it for $4,500 or so. That gives us the profit of $1,500 we're looking for.

If we spend $2,000 on the bike, invest another $1,000 to get it up to our standard, then we have invested a total of $3,000. If we sell it for $4,500 then we profit $1,500. That's a 50% return on our investment. Considering the whole process takes about a month, that's a tremendous return for a 30-day investment!

The bikes we're going to sell are at a price point that attracts the most buyers. They are relatively inexpensive. They are not $40,000 vintage, fully customized Harley-Davidson choppers. They are Honda Shadows, and Suzuki Boulevards, and Kawasaki Vulcans that are priced in the $2,500 - $5,500 range.

Year

We want to find bikes that were made in the year 2000 or newer. There are two reasons for this.

First, there is psychology in play here. A 1998 bike seems like it was made a lifetime ago versus a 2000 model. In reality, there is only a 2-year difference and both bikes are over 20 years old! But, something about the "19" makes a bike seem like it is ancient.

Second, the value of a bike is based more on its condition and less on the number of miles.[4] Things age and deteriorate over time. The year 2000 is a good cutoff point on the age of all the components of a bike. Even at this age, there will be several components that need to be inspected and possibly replaced. We'll go over that more later. Also, the internals of the engine start to be called into question if you get too much older than this.

4.2 Prepurchase Analysis

Once you have found a few bikes that meet your sourcing filter it's time to contact some sellers and do some investigative work.

When we contact a seller, we are trying to accomplish a prepurchase analysis to see if the bike is a good choice.

We need to:

- Learn the bike's story
- Decide if the problems it has are acceptable or unacceptable

- Conduct a VIN Check
- Create a draft budget

Like people, every bike is going to have a story. It is important that we investigate the bike's story before we buy it. The story will tell us what the general condition of the bike is. Our job, the value we bring, is to fix the problem and give the bike a new chapter in its story. We're looking for bikes with stories and therefore are selling for deeply discounted, "wholesale" prices. We buy them at wholesale prices, refurbish them, and resale them at retail prices.

This leads to another question—what if the bike doesn't really have a story and doesn't really have any problems? If that's the case, then you probably can't buy it for a wholesale price. If you can, then I would question if maybe the bike does have a story and you just don't know what it is—it's a lemon and too good to be true. Bike listed at wholesale prices have a story to tell.

We want bikes with stories to tell and are listed at wholesale, deeply discounted prices. As it turns out, bikes will generally fall into four categories—four stories. One of these is a bike we'll avoid, and the other three are what we're looking for. I've given them silly names to help you remember them.

Acceptable Problems

Neglected Nelly

Neglected Nelly's are bikes that have been parked for a long period of time—typically years. They may or may not have had gas in their tanks and fuel systems when they were parked. If they did, it has all evaporated and left a mess. Their carburetors or fuel injectors are all gummed up with the gooey, sticky stuff that evaporated gas leaves behind. Because of this, they won't start. Their tires and batteries are out of date. They're covered in a patina of dirt and possibly rust. To their divorcing owner, they are a useless hunk of nothing. But we know better.

Neglected Nelly's are great bikes to flip, and I highly recommend them. The reason is because they generally don't have maintenance issues other than the effects of being left untouched for a couple years. They worked fine when they were parked. For whatever reason (death, lack of interest, etc.), they were just neglected. Neglected Nelly's are a great find.

Broken Betty

Broken Betty's are bikes that worked great until something, one thing, broke. Maybe it was a shifter cable, maybe it was one of the EFI sensors, maybe something in the charging system. Who knows? But it's just that one thing. Other than that, the bike is in great shape. What usually happens is that the one thing broke, the owner got a bid from a mechanic to fix it and decided to just sell it. It all happened in the course of a few weeks, so Broken Betty's are usually not also Neglected Nelly's (but sometimes they are).

Here's the thing about Broken Betty's. If the problem is somewhat known, you can do quite a bit of research beforehand to determine what kind of project its going to be to fix it. There's always that risk that the problem ends up being something other than what you though it was. So, do your research for sure.

Broken Betty's are great because a lot of times you don't have the additional cost of having to replace tires, the battery, etc. All that stuff was being maintained up until the point of the failure.

A note here, be leery of Broken Betty with internal engine problems. For the purposes of the Moneybike formula, think of the engine as all one component and it's the most expensive. It either works or it doesn't. If the problem is something internal to the engine, I would pass.

Dropsy Daisy

Dropsy Daisies are bikes that have tipped over. The key here is that they were dropped *while not in motion*. In other words, the bike was not traveling down the road and it tipped over.

One day, I was working on a bike. I had it up on a jack, but in my hurry, I didn't tie it down to the jack. I was doing something to the bike that was jarring it and it fell off the jack (away from me thank goodness). The bike became a Dropsy Daisy. Luckily for me, I only managed to do about $85 in damage to the bike! It was an $85 lesson well learned.

Dropsy Daisies are great because generally they don't have any other maintenance issues except busted stuff on one side. What you want to be careful of is a dented tank. Not all Dropsy Daisies have dented tanks. It all depends on the circumstances of the drop. In my example, the bike had an engine guard that prevented the tank from being dented.

If the bike has a dented tank, then you'll need to make sure to get an estimate from a body shop to fix it, or research if you can do it yourself. That is the big hassle that is causing the seller to get rid of it. That's the hassle we're signing up to correct and make our profit.

Unacceptable Problems

Sideswipe Sally

Stay away from Sideswipe Sally's. These are bikes that have been dropped during a moving accident. The bike was involved in an accident, the rider laid it down, and the whole side of the bike has damage.

Sideswipe Sally's take a lot of money repair (eating up our profits). Also, since they've been involved in a moving accident, there is a chance that other problems exist. These could be as severe as dented frames, or wheels, or forks. The point is, there are so many bikes to choose from that we don't have to settle for Sideswipe Sally. So, we pass and find another one.

VIN Check

Before you drive to see the bike in person, you should always run a VIN check. The VIN is like the serial number for the motorcycle. This number is referenced if the bike has had any major incident such as an accident, if it was involved in a flood, vandalism, or if it has been reported as stolen. You need to make sure you check the VIN for any of these complications. If the VIN comes back as stolen, then you probably need to contact law enforcement.

There are a few ways to check the VIN. I recommend doing two things. First, some states have a free website to check if the VIN has been reported as stolen. Colorado, for example, has a website that allows you to add in the VIN and see if it was reported as stolen. If this is an option for the state that the bike has a title, then do this first.

Second, there are paid services that check state databases, insurance databases, and Federal databases. Below is a list of websites that provide this service. *Never* buy a bike without checking out the VIN with one of these services. They are inexpensive and worth every penny.

- Clearvin.com
- Titlecheck.us
- Vinaudit.com
- Vindatahistory.com

If the VIN checks out good, and in talking with the seller you are confident that the condition of the bike is what was listed, then you should travel to see the bike in person.

Draft Budget

At this point you know enough about the condition of the bike to create a draft budget. This budget is just an estimate and tells you how much profit you can expect to make.

You should have a good understanding of all the expenses. Total costs include:

- Cost of the bike
- Tax, Title and Registration Fees
- Transportation fees (as applicable)
- Tires
- Oil and oil filter
- Spark plugs
- Battery
- Major components that must be replaced
- Brake pads
- Bike cover (I always include a bike cover)
- Extra key and keychains
- Extras such as upgraded grips, mirrors, saddlebags, windshield, etc.
- CycleTrader Advertisement
- Fuel for test riding
- OEM bits and pieces ($50 or so for this)

Here is an example budget. There are several others at the end of this book in the case studies.

Item	Estimate
Initial Purchase	
Purchase Price	$ 2,000.00
Online VIN Check	$ 15.00
Tax, Title, Registration	$ 215.00
Transportation	$ 100.00
Parts & Restoration	
Tires ($25/ea to mount and balance)	$ 350.00
Oil & Filter	$ 20.00
Spark Plug(s)	$ 6.00
Battery	$ 100.00
Misc OEM bits	$ 50.00
Extras (Optional)	
Bike Cover	$ 30.00
Keychains	$ 12.00
Rear fender bib	$ 100.00
Fuel for test riding	$ 25.00
CycleTrader Ad	$ 30.00
Total Cost	$ 3,053.00
Sales Price	$ 4,600.00
Profit	$ 1,547.00
Margin	33.63%
ROI	50.67%

4.3 In-Person Inspection

Coordinate a time and place with the seller to see the bike. Many times, the bike is not drivable. So, you will need to meet the seller at their residence. Keep in mind that the bike is in an unknown condition. That being the case, you never want to ride the bike back home. Don't risk it. Bring a trailer, or in my case, pay a family member to use their trailer. That's the safest way to transport a bike back home. I pay an uncle $2 per mile to transport bikes from the location of purchase back to my home. I figure that cost into my budget. It's a good source of revenue for him and it's a great service for me.

You will need to conduct a "Pre-Purchase Bike Inspection" when you see the bike for the first time. The intent of this inspection is to identify if there are any issues with the bike that you weren't already aware of. Hopefully, you have already talked to the seller, and you know if the bike needs new tires, a fresh battery, and so forth. This pre-purchase inspection is to identify any surprises and then adjust your offer accordingly.

One time I showed up at a home to purchase a bike and found out the bike didn't have a muffler. Surprise! It wasn't a showstopper at all, but I did adjust my offer down by $200 to compensate for it.

The second big goal of the pre-purchase inspection is to ensure that the VIN stamped on the frame of the bike is the same VIN as on the Title document. Sometimes, folks will steal a bike and attempt to sell it with a fraudulent title, or some other bike's title. Always visually check the VIN on the frame (the "neck" of the bike under the handlebars) versus the Title document.

Below is the prepurchase checklist that I have successfully used many times.

Item
Front tire - manufacturer date, tread depth
Front wheel - any obvious bending or malformities
Front brakes - check disk and caliper area for leaks, check pad depth, ops check front brakes
Forks - check trueness, check for leaky seals
Headlight - ops check
Front turn signals - ops check
Horn - ops check
Clutch - Is it bent or marred? How does it feel?
Master Cylinder - check for leaks, fluid level
Rear view mirrors - anything damaged or missing?
Gas tank - dents?
Speedometer - dents, cracks, etc.
Seats - any rips?
Rear blinkers - ops check
Rear brake like - ops check
Rear tire - manufacturers date, tread depth
Rear wheel - any obvious bending or malformities
Engine - visible damage? Anything missing?
Left foot controls (clutch) - anything missing?
Right foot controls (rear brake) - anything missing? Rear brake ops check
Exhaust headers and mufflers - anything missing or damaged?
Kick stand - present and functional?
VIN Check - Compare VIN on frame with VIN on Title document
Accessories (Windshield, bags, etc.) - ops check and general condition

At this point you should have accomplished the following:

- Checked the VIN using 1 or more online services
- Contacted the seller to understand the bike's story and confirm its condition
- Traveled to see the bike in person
- Verified the condition of the bike in person
- Verified the VIN on the bike versus the Title

4.4 Purchase the Moneybike

We've done our due diligence and have decided that this is the bike for us. It is time to consummate the transaction! The paperwork involved will be:

- Buyer and Seller signing the back of the Title
- Buyer and Seller signing a bill of sale
- (State dependent) Buyer and Seller signing tax and registration document required by taxing office

Sign the paperwork, fork over the cash, and load up your new Moneybike!

4.5 Refurbish the Moneybike

In this section we will cover the Moneybike Standard and the Moneybike Gameplan. The standard is where we want our bike to be once we're done. The Moneybike gameplan gets us there.

The Moneybike Standard

To review, we've found our bikes using our sourcing filter, we've conducted a prepurchase analysis, we've traveled to the location of the bike and did an in-person inspection, we've purchased the bike and transported it home. Now, we need to bring the bike up to our Moneybike standard.

The "Moneybike Standard" means the condition of the bike is immaculate. It's a finished product, ready to be sold at a retail price.

The following requirements detail what The Moneybike Standard looks like. However, the general theme is that when you sell the bike the only thing the new owner needs to do is ride the heck out of it!

Maintenance – All maintenance issues have been corrected. Any broken items have been fixed

Oil and Filter – new oil and new oil filter

Spark Plugs – Always install new spark plugs. I don't care if the previous owner just changed them, spend $6 and put new ones in. If anything, it becomes a $6 selling point you can place on your ad, "New spark plugs".

Gear Oil – Only shaft drive bikes will have gear oil. If so, go ahead and put fresh gear oil in. This is another low cost, easy to do item that gives you another great selling point on your ad

Brake Pads – Most brake pads have wear indicators. If they are worn past them (or even close), replace them. Front pads take the brunt of breaking and will require replacing at least twice as much as rear.

BATTERY – motorcycle batteries last about 3 years give or take. Anything older than that and you'll want to replace it.

TIRES – This will be one of your biggest costs. If the tires are beyond their manufacturer's lifespan (typically 5 years), or if the tread is close to the wear indicators, then you'll want to replace them. Bikes with spoke rims also have tubes and rim strips. They get replaced along with the tires. New tires on a bike are a huge selling point. Rarely will I leave tires on the bike that it came with. Also, this gives me a chance to change the look of the bike if I want to by replace all black tires with whitewalls or vice versa. New tires are a huge selling point and separate you from other bikes listed. Look at what's listed on Facebook and try to find a motorcycle with brand new front and rear tires—it's rare.

FORK SEALS – The fork seals should not be leaking. This is one of those issues that is easy to spot. Look at the front forks and if you see dirt rings a few inches below where the top fork and bottom fork meet then you might have a leak. If you do a little research, you'll quickly be able to spot leaking fork seals.

OEM BITS AND PIECES – You may find that previous owners have used hardware store screws in the place of OEM nuts and bolts. Or you might find that various fasteners and small components are missing. We want to make sure that all OEM bits and pieces are installed on the bike unless there is a specific reason. For example, some bikes have replaced the passenger seat with a decorative leather tank bib. That's fine. But, if there is a rubber grommet missing that helps hold a plastic fairing piece in place, we need to put it on our parts list to order. Most of the time, these OEM bits and pieces don't amount to very much cost at all. But, having them ensures the bike comes across as a finished product.

BIKE DETAILED – You will need to wash the bike a few times through the course of refurbish process. The initial bike wash will be to remove most of the dirt and gunk that can prevent you from seeing any leaks or other defects. Later in the process, you'll get quite a bit more detailed and continue to clean the bike. The final product should be spotless. Not a spec of dirt seen anywhere on the bike.

CORROSION – Use Magic Blue, Mothers, or similar product to remove rust. There is an awesome product called "Blue Job" that works very well on metal chrome surfaces that have rusted. I use Magic Blue mainly and bring out the heavy-duty Blue Job for the really tough jobs. Blue Job also takes exhaust pipes that have discolored to yellow/blue and restores them to a Chrome finish. It's a great product.

PAINTED SURFACES – Most of the time you can bring back the glory of painted surfaces by washing them and then using Turtle Wax products.

CHROME – Again, I use Magic Blue or Mothers for general chrome polishing. Get that chrome looking nice. Motorcycles have lots of chrome and when it's spiffed up it really makes the bike look like a piece of artwork.

RUBBER/BLACK PLASTIC – Mothers and Turtle Wax both have products to restore black plastic or black rubber components that have faded. You can use these products on the rubber surfaces of foot controls, black plastic on odometer components, fuel lines, coolant lines, and anything else that is black.

LIGHTING – Ensure the headlights, high beams, turn signals and brake lights all function correctly. You'll probably need to do this for your state safety inspection anyhow.

HORN – Ensure the horn functions correctly. Again, this is probably a state safety inspection requirement.

INSTRUMENT CLUSTER – Instrument clusters have various functions in addition to tracking miles ridden and your current speed. You'll want to ensure the speedometer works, gas gauge (if equipped) works, and any other functionality is operational.

KEYS – To further separate us in the marketplace, we want two (2) sets of keys with nice, new keychains. Branded keychains can be found on Amazon or eBay for dirt cheap. Hopefully you have at least one key for the bike. You can get a spare key a couple of different ways. The expensive way is to look it up on the illustrated parts breakdown (keys are usually on the wiring harness drawing). Those are $20 - $40 typically. A less expensive option is to simply purchase a key blank from eBay. Let me explain a little about how our motorcycle keys work. First, they are usually two sided. This means that they are cut on both sides. Second, you'll want to pay special attention to the groves of your existing key and make sure your key blank has the same grove pattern. Here's a picture of a motorcycle key and it's groove pattern:

You can get key blanks on eBay for a fraction of the price so long as you get the correct groove pattern. Use the following search phrase in eBay's search bar, replacing the year and model of the motorcycle in question:

"2005 Suzuki Boulevard C50 key blank"

Once you have the key blank, you'll need to get someone to cut it. Mom and pop hardware stores usually have a key duplicating service. For a couple bucks you can get them to cut your key. Another, more expensive option, is to purchase your own key duplicator for around $280 on Amazon. Use the following search phrase on Amazon to see these devices:

"key duplicator machine"

TITLE DOCUMENT – A title is the most important document in a motorcycle sale. It is the certificate which confirms the motorcycle ownership status. I say all this because Facebook is littered with people trying to sell bikes without titles. Please beware that it is illegal to sell a motorcycle (or any automobile) in many states without a title. It's not just a bad idea, but it's actually against the law in a lot of circumstances. If the seller doesn't have a title, then how do you know they own it in the first place? You don't. The title could have been lost in a move, eaten by the family dog, or the bike could have been stolen from some poor schmuck in Wisconsin. You just don't know which is the case! Never buy a car or motorcycle without a title. For that reason, we need to make sure we have a clear title, in our name, ready to go for the buyer. Again, we're setting our bike apart as a finished product.

ENHANCEMENTS ADDED – I like to spend $50 to $100 to add some new stuff to the bike. Maybe I add a rear fender bib, or a handmade leather tank bib found on Etsy. Maybe I upgrade the stock grips to some awesome chrome grips found on eBay. Maybe I upgrade the mirrors. I try to add 1 or 2 brand new things to the bike.

It's a selling point and helps to separate the bike from all the other listings.

BIKE COVER – I always sell my bikes with a brand-new bike cover. These are inexpensive and run about $30 on Amazon. This is another selling point to separate our bike from the competition in the marketplace.

So that's what the "Moneybike Standard" means. We do all those things. At the end of it, the bike is a finished product. It's 100% fixed, polished, and in great shape—ready for its new rider.

Do yourself a favor here and keep track of all the selling points. Here's an example of what your list of selling points should look like:

> **Selling Points:**
>
> - Clear Title in my name
> - Current State inspection
> - Extremely low mileage
> - Starts right up
> - Fuel injected
> - Fuel injectors cleaned, tested
> - Smooth shifting transmission
> - Hard Krome Res-Tec 3" Performance Drag Pipes; Feature patented True Doublewall Construction; Aftermarket performance exhaust pipes that sound AWESOME (this was a $900 upgrade)
> - Liquid cooled
> - Driver floorboards
> - Heel toe shifter
> - Windshield with Boulevard emblem
> - Studded leather saddlebags with Boulevard emblem
> - Studded leather seats
> - Studded leather passenger seat
> - Studded leather sissy bar with back support
> - Passenger pegs
> - Classic white-faced instrument gauge
> - Two tone classic paint scheme
> - New rear whitewall tire, tube & rim strip
> - New front whitewall tire, tube & rim strip
> - Completely cleaned and flushed fuel system

Keeping track of your selling points along the way is much easier than trying to remember everything at the time of creating your listing.

The Moneybike Gameplan

The Moneybike Gameplan is the list of tasks, in sequential order, that need to be accomplished to bring your bike up to the Moneybike Standard previously discussed.

The Moneybike Gameplan details what needs to be accomplished, and in what order. The Moneybike Gameplan has 4 phases.

PHASE 1 – DISASSEMBLE, INSPECT, ORDER PARTS: The goal here is to identify all the parts necessary and get them on order. Parts take time to ship so you want to do this soon. Other phase 1 tasks include the first bike wash and basic inspections. The goal here is to get a complete picture of what all needs to be accomplished on the bike. At the end of phase 1, you should have all the parts on order that you're going to need and have a good understand of the work that needs to be accomplished to complete the bike.

PHASE 2 – PREPARE FOR SAFETY INSPECTION: In my state, a motorcycle must pass a safety inspection. The bike must be drivable and just about everything needs to be functional to pass this inspection. This is where we're fixing any mechanical issues, doing the basic maintenance actions such as an oil change, waking the engine up if it's a Neglected Nelly, and so on.

Engine Wakeup

If you're dealing with a Neglected Nelly, you want to wake the engine up slowly. It's a simple process and I've talked with very experience mechanics who say this is absolutely the thing to do for an engine that's been sitting idle for years on end.

This is a good procedure to do when you're changing spark plugs. Here's what you do.

1. Gain access to the internal combustion chamber of each cylinder by removing the spark plugs. Be sure to follow your maintenance manual when you remove the plugs.
2. Pour in a capful of Marvel Mystery Oil. This is the stuff that looks like fruit punch. Use a long funnel and pour it right in the hole where the spark plug was.
3. Add some Sea Foam. If using aerosol, hold the red straw so it doesn't shoot off the cap and go into the spark plug hole. Add a shot glass full of Sea Foam, or a couple squirts, into the combustion chamber.
4. Manually rotate the engine. You'll need to research how to do this and follow your maintenance manual. Basically, you're accessing a nut on the left side by removing a cover, then

using a 17mm socket and large wrench to manually rotate the engine in a counterclockwise direction (the same direction that the tires rotate when the bike is moving forward). Again, use your maintenance manual. The idea here is that by manually rotating the engine, the pistons move up and down, smearing your oil/sea foam concoction all over the walls of the internal combustion chamber.
5. At this point, you should let the bike sit for a day or so. I usually do this procedure when I know I won't be firing it up for the first time for a while. It's like soaking a cake pan--the longer you let it sit the better.

When you attempt the start the bike for the first time, just know that it's going to burn all that stuff out of the combustion chamber and produce a little smoke for a few minutes. That's perfectly normal.

Other Milestone 2 tasks include inspecting and changing fluids, fixing broken things, reassembling with OEM parts, adding the bike to your insurance policy, and some test riding.

Test Rides

In Phase 2, you still test ride the bike for the first time. A discussion is warranted here on test riding a bike for the first time. Safety is paramount. The bike may not have been ridden for a while, so you need to take steps to mitigate risks and slowly build confidence in the bike. Here's how I do that.

When test riding a Moneybike for the first time:

- Wear all the gear—The Full Monty. Wear your protective jacket, full face helmet, gloves, jeans, boots—the whole shebang.
- Inspect the bike again using the Motorcycle Safety Foundation T-CLOCS Checklist – Tires, Controls, Lights, Oil, Chassis, Stands [5]
- Build confidence slowly. Start with a slow (20mph) ride around the neighborhood. Is everything in working order and adjusted? Brakes good, etc.? Next, go around the block (30mph). If everything checks out at this speed, then take it out to a local state highway and ride in the 60mph range.

Build confidence in the bike slowly and carefully, listening for issues and problem along the way.

As a part of your test riding, you might need a state safety inspection. Get that done and then register the bike with your local tax office. For me, it's a 10-day waiting period between registering the bike and when my new Title shows up the mail. Just enough time to put some miles on the bike and make sure it's in great condition.

PHASE 3 – PREPARE FOR LISTING: In phase 3, we are completing the tasks to get the bike ready to sell. These tasks include new tires and breaks (if necessary), adjusting the controls for drivability, and a more thorough detailing of the bike. At the end of phase 3, the bike should be in pristine condition and ready to be presented to prospective buyers.

PHASE 4 – SELL BIKE: In this phase we're taking pictures of the bike, creating the listing on Facebook and CycleTrader, showing the bike to prospective buyers, negotiating, and finally selling the bike.

The table below is a good example of a complete Moneybike gameplan. Start with this table and modify as you see fit.

Phase 1 - Disassemble, inspect, order parts
Research specs - tire sizes, carb info, other specs that will be referred to often during the build
1st bike wash
Inspect bike and put together parts list to order
Gas Tank - remove, inspect, clean
Air Cleaner - disassemble, inspect
Seats - remove, inspect
Battery - remove, inspect, recharge
Fuel Rails - inspect
Fuel Injectors - remove, inspect, test, clean
Fork Frame Covers - remove, inspect
Frame Covers - remove, inspect
Tool Kit - remove, inspect, inventory
Fuses (under seat and near coolant reservoir) - remove, inspect
Chrome valve covers - remove, polish & detail (easier while tank is off)
Fork Seals - inspect
Turn signals, brake light, headlight, license plate light, horn - test, inspect
Order parts
Milestone 1 - Bike disassembled and parts are on order

Phase 2 - Prepare for State Safety Inspection
Add Marvel Mystery oil to cylinders
Manually rotate engine
Change final drive (gear) oil
Blow out air filter with compressed air
Replace spark plugs
Change oil, filter
Inspect, fill coolant as necessary
Reassembly bike with all OEM parts ordered in Phase 1
Add bike to insurance policy
Test Ride!
State safety inspection
Register bike with tax office
Milestone 2 - Bike inspected and registered

Phase 3 - Prepare for Listing
Remove wheels and replace tires
Remove/inspect front brake cylinder and pads
Remove/inspect rear brake drums
Test ride for a while
Adjust controls as necessary
2nd bike wash and detail
Take Pics
Milestone 3 - Bike ready for listing

Phase 4 - Sell Bike
Add listing to Facebook and CycleTrader
Negotiate and sell bike
Milestone 4 - Sold!

4.6 List on Facebook and CycleTrader

We list the bike on Facebook Marketplace, Facebook local buy and sell groups, and CycleTrader.com. The goal here is exposure. Our bike's new owner is out there and it's our job to find them. To do that we need as many eyeballs on our listing as possible.

Our listing needs to stand out from the crowd on these websites. So, we need to make sure of a few things.

High Quality Pictures

You need 20 high-quality pictures. You can get the quality you need with the cell phone you probably already own. You don't need to invest in any special camera. Your phone is good enough. Do the following to take high quality pictures:

- Take your photos during the "magic hour" of the day. This is 30 minutes before sunset. The sun is low in the sky giving you an abundance of natural light.
- Express the dream! In other words, the context of the picture is important. Find a spot where your bike looks great. For me, it's a local lake and really cool downtown area. Motorcycles look awesome in those two settings.

- Use Google Photos, or similar software, to enhance your photos. The free software (like Google Photos) is all you need. It does a great job.
- Take pictures from every angle. You want to show all sides of your bike.
- Don't focus on cosmetic blemishes. Here's the thing. You want to be honest with your prospective buyers. But be smart about it and time it correctly. When they come over to see the bike in person, and you remove the cover, and they gasp because the bike looks awesome, that's the right time to show them the scuff on the rear fender. Not when they are looking at limited info on Facebook or CycleTrader.
- Stay out of your pics. Don't put people (or yourself) in the pictures. Nobody wants to see you; they want to see the bike. Your Moneybike will have a lot of chrome that's all polished up, so be mindful of reflections as well.
- Fill 80% of the frame with your bike. Don't zoom in, move in. Zooming decreases the quality of the picture. So, just take a few steps closer to ensure the bike fills up 80% of the frame.

High Quality Listing

Your listing needs to be a high quality as well. That means you want to put a lot of detail in the listing. You did a lot of working turning your project into a Moneybike and you want to communicate that in your listing. What you're basically trying to say is, "I've taken care of everything. The bike is ready to go!".

Here is an example of a high-quality listing:

2007 Suzuki Boulevard C50 – Completely Refurbished!

This one-of-a-kind bike has been 100% inspected, refurbished and ready for its new rider.

Title and Licensing:

I have a clean, blue Texas title in hand for this bike. A title is the most important document in a motorcycle sale. It is the certificate which confirms the motorcycle ownership status. I say all this because Facebook is littered with people trying to sell bikes without titles. Please beware that it is illegal to sell a motorcycle (or any automobile) in the State of Texas without a title. It's not just a bad idea, but it's against the law. If the seller doesn't have a title, then how do you know they own it in the first place? You don't. The title could have been lost in a move, eaten by the family dog, or the bike could have been stolen from some poor schmuck in Wisconsin. You just don't know which is the case! Never buy a car or motorcycle without a title.

The Best Starter to Intermediate Bike You Can Find:

These Suzuki Boulevards are legendary and have a very active following of riders online. There is a ton of information on the internet about various modifications and improvements for this bike, how to operate it, and how to maintain it. This bike is powerful enough to be fun, but still manageable for a brand-new rider. It is not too heavy, and it is low to the ground. This makes it easy for new riders to handle and to confidently sit flat footed while stopped. Intermediate riders will enjoy the power that the 800cc engine provides. This bike can easily cruise along FM roads, Texas state highways, and even the interstate. The custom paint and styling on this bike is very unique and most definitely turns heads.

The perfect bike for the daily commuter:

The fuel mileage for this bike is about 42 miles per gallon. That makes this bike the perfect solution for someone looking for an inexpensive daily rider. Let's do some commuter math:

This bike has a 4-gallon gas tank.

4 gallons x $3.90 per gallon = $15.60. So, a tank of gas will cost you about $15 bucks

Each tank of gas will get you about 160 miles down the road (42 miles per gallon x 4 gallons, minus a little bit since you don't actually burn every ounce of fuel before refilling). If your commute is 10 miles to work, or 20 miles each day, then you will get about 8 days of riding for each tank of gas. That means you'll need to fill up 3.75 times per month (30 / 8). So, this bike will cost you about $56 bucks per month—not $56 per fill-up like our cars do now! Realistically, you'll probably spend twice that on gas. This is because you'll fill it up on Saturday mornings and burn the whole tank zooming around Texas all weekend because this bike is so much fun to ride!

Refurb Details:

Every inch of this bike has been cleaned and inspected. The bike was purchased with only 11k miles on it. The 300 or so miles over and above that is from my test riding. Everything that failed inspection was fixed or replaced. Everything that cropped up during test rides was fixed or replaced. The intent was to restore this bike to its original condition, ready for its new rider.

Here is a list of what was accomplished:

- Front tire inspected good - plenty of tread and is well within manufacturer's suggested age
- New rear tire, inner tube, and rim strip
- New spark plugs (x 2)

- K&N Air filter has been completely cleaned and service (remember, K&Ns don't get replaced, they get cleaned and are design to last the lifetime of your bike)
- Battery install date is February 2020; It has been inspected and tested good
- Gas tank cleaned internally and inspected
- Brand new OEM fuel pump assembly and O-ring installed in gas tank
- Brand new OEM fuel sending unit installed in gas tank
- Both fuel injectors professionally cleaned
- Throttle body cleaned and inspected
- Paint touched up where needed
- Oil changed with new filters
- Completely detailed front to back
    - Everything cleaned
    - All chrome polished
    - All painted surfaces touched up and protected with turtle wax

Extras:

This bike is loaded with extras:

- Custom paint job
- Aftermarket custom drag style handlebars – I'm tall (6'6") and these bars are very comfortable! They look great too
- Aftermarket Chrome handlebar grips
- K&N Air Filter – guaranteed by K&N to last the lifetime of the bike
- New all-weather bike cover – No garage? No problem. This cover does a great job protecting the bike from the elements.
- Driver floorboards – these make a huge difference in riding comfort
- Chrome heel / toe shifter
- Engine guard / highway bars
- Passenger seat, pegs, and sissy bar
- Memphis Shades high end windshield mounts
- 2 Keys w/ Leather keychains

This bike is ready to commute around town, explore Texas—or journey through the heartland of America!

Delivery:

Yes! I will deliver for a reasonable fee of $2 per mile from my house (calculated 1 way). So, if you're 80 miles away the delivery fee would be $160.

Test rides:

You bet you can test ride it! Test rides are available under the following conditions:

- Riders have a valid Texas driver's license with a motorcycle endorsement
- Riders have their own helmet and eye protection
- Riders must have purchase price, in cash, to be held by seller during test ride

My Facebook Ground Rules:

- If you are reading this then yes, the bike is still for sale. When I sell the bike, I promise I will take this ad down within 2 nanoseconds. So, if it's up, it's for sale.
- No, I won't respond to "Is this still Available"? Sorry, but too many malicious bots use this. So, it's now a useless function for us humans who just want to buy and sell stuff. Just tell me your name, where you're from, and ask any questions you may have or ask when you can see the bike.
- No, I won't respond to any codes, give you my social security number, credit card number or do any other stupid things to get myself hacked or defrauded.
- No, I won't hold the bike for anyone--unless you're a friend. If you're a friend, then you bet I'll hold it for you. If you're a stranger, then you're outa luck and you'd better setup a time to see it as soon as you can before another buyer gets it!

And finally,

"Motorcycles are bought, never sold. Bought by people who know exactly what they want and are unlikely to be weaned from their fixations by the actions of salesmen." -Bert Hopwood, British motorcycle designer

In other words, if this is your bike, you'll know it.

This listing has a ton of detail. Facebook Marketplace doesn't have a maximum length that I'm aware of. So, we will make use of that! The buyers want to see as much detail as possible about the bike when browsing motorcycles. Now let's talk a little about pricing.

Pricing

Our Moneybikes are going to be in perfect shape. As such, we should price them at the upper range of their estimated value. Kelly Blue Book and NADA are both great websites to assess value. Here's what I usually do to assess value.

First, look the bike up on Kelly Blue Book. My price is typically $100 - $500 over this amount. The KBB price assumes average condition. Our Moneybikes are well above average and command a premium price.

Next, look the bike up on CycleTrader and Facebook to see what the competition is going for. You'll find that CycleTrader bikes are at the upper end of the price spectrum, but the bikes are in great condition. Facebook is a crapshoot. What you're basically trying to figure out is, what is the range of prices.

Go on CycleTrader and list the prices for all the bikes of similar make and model, in a 100-mile radius. That graph should look something like this:

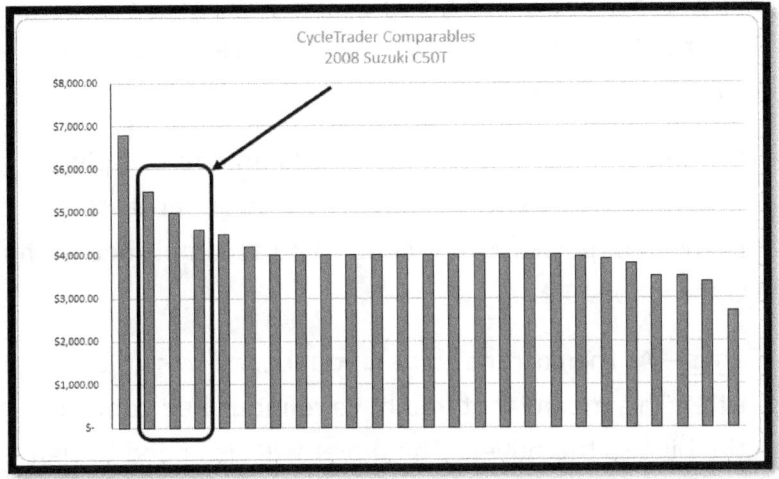

This is actual data from one of my bikes that will be in the Case Studies section below. In the chart above, each blue bar is a bike on CycleTrader that is the same year model as my Moneybike. The range of prices show that most bikes were selling around $4,000. I priced this bike at $5,200 and it sold for $4,800. You can see, it was priced at the upper end of the spectrum and that's where it sold. Our bikes are premium because of the work we do to restore them. They should be priced accordingly.

4.7 Negotiating and Selling

Have your bottom dollar in mind before talking to your first buyer. Remember, we're shooting for 50% ROI. So that means if you've invested $2,800 in the bike then you're looking to make $1,400 in profit. That means your bottom dollar is $4,200 and you've probably set the initial price at $4,400.

When you've landed on a price, it's time to complete the transaction with the buyer. There are at least two items of paperwork that need to be accomplished in the transaction.

TITLE – As the current owner, you'll need to sign the title. This means that you have relinquished control of the bike to the buyer. The buyer will also need to sign the title as well.

BILL OF SALE – In addition to signing the title (and not in lieu of!), you need to complete bill of sale. The bill of sale is another document that provides evidence that the ownership of the bike changed from you to the buyer. Always complete the bill of sale in addition to the title. It's a good document that shows possession has changed from you to them. You never know what the new buyer is going to do with their motorcycle. You need documentation showing that you sold the bike to them, and possession transferred.

There may be other documents to complete as well depending on your state. For example, in Texas we complete a 130-U form that both the buyer and seller sign. This form is used at the tax office when registering the bike. Check with your local tax office for any additional documents.

5 Setting up Shop

Now that we're familiar with The Moneybike Formula it's time to setup shop and get started. You'll need to do a few things to prepare for your very first Moneybike.

When setting up shop it is very easy to go overboard and spend too much money. Don't do that. Your mantra for setting up shop is "less is more, use what you have". Don't buy all the special tools you think you MAY need, buy them as you DO need them ("tool acquisition opportunities" as I refer to them).

There are a few basics that you're going to need. Everything else can be acquired as a part of your projects.

5.1 Work Area

You're going to need some physical space to work. You need flooring that can handle the occasional oil or fuel spill. You need enough lighting to be able to work in the evenings. You need an area, out of the weather, for your bike as you work to refurbish it. You'll also need storage for parts that are removed from the bike. You need a place for your tools and shop supplies.

In other words, you need something like a residential garage which works perfectly. A standard garage gives you everything you'll need for your work area. A shed, a shop, and even a carport are also very good options.

Stay organized. You don't want to waste time looking for tools. Every tool should have a place. When you buy a new tool, you have a decision to make—where will this new tool live? Thrown in the drawer with a bunch of other tools is not a good option. Remember, we're trying to make as much profit using as little of our labor as possible. If you spend a bunch of time looking for tools because your disorganized, then you aren't making the money per hour that you could be. Stay organized!

Organize your work area into categories to save time. Hand tools over there. Power tools over here. Safety equipment such as safety glasses and latex gloves go there. Wrenches are here, sockets over there. That kind of thing. Use categories so you can quickly find the tools you're looking for.

Label all your areas to save time. If you have shelves, with boxes of stuff that sit on those shelves, then use labels on the boxes. That way, you don't have to waste time digging through the box to see if something is or is not in it. Use labels to save time.

Start with a basic set of tools. Here's a list of the very basic tools that you will probably need for your first bike:

- SAE & metric socket set
- SAE & metric bit socks
- Screwdriver set
- Regular, diagonal cutting and long nose pliers
- SAE & metric combination wrench set
- SAE & metric hex key set
- Extension bars and adapters
- Ratchets and universal joint adapter set

A quick look at the Harbor Freight website shows that a 301 Piece Mechanics Tool Set runs $219.99. That's perfect and all you need to get started.

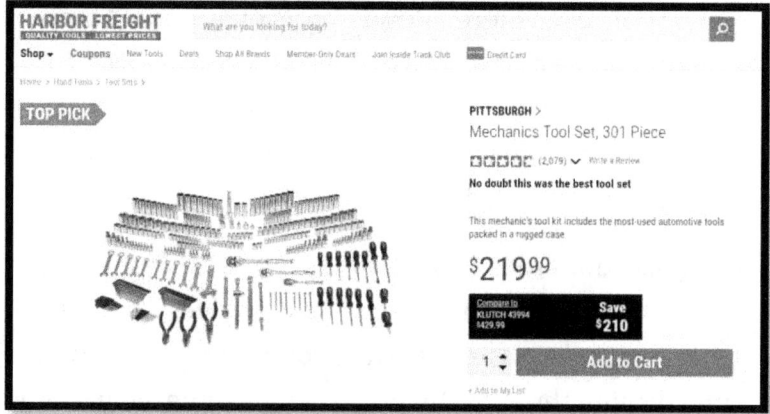

Another item that makes things much easier is a motorcycle jack and a set of ratchet straps. Working on motorcycles is infinitely easier when it's securely up on a jack. It's not mandatory, but it really helps. Again, Harbor Freight has a great option here:

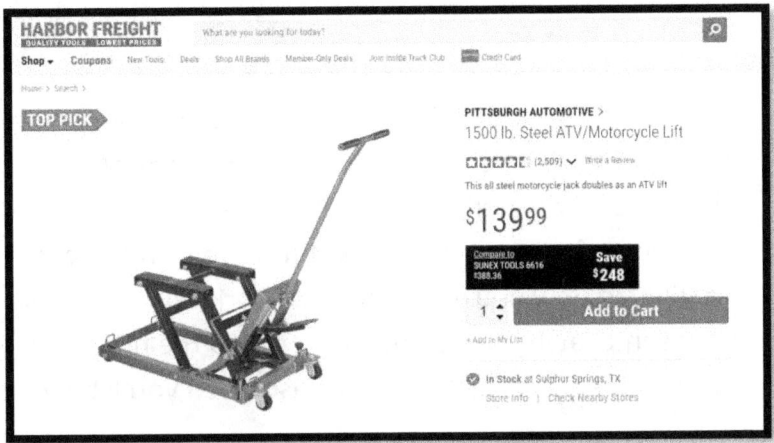

Additional supplies that you should have on hand include:

- Safety goggles
- Latex gloves
- Protective leather gloves (the cheap ones from Lowes are fine)
- Oil rags and detailing rags (old t-shirts work fine)

That's pretty much it for your work area. Again, the rule of thumb here is to only purchase what you need. If you need anything special, factor that into the cost of the project bike you are working on. For example, one of my special tools I needed was a long-stemmed hex bit set. Instead of buying this up front, I waited until I needed it and factored it into the cost of the bike I was working on at the time.

5.2 Starting Capital

You'll need about $2,000 to $3,000 of cash to get started. This will be used to purchase the bike along with the other expenses to get it through the Moneybike formula. If you don't have this on-hand, be creative on how you get it. Maybe work extra hours, mow some lawns, sell some junk around the house. If you can pile up about $3,000 in cash, then you'll be in business.

5.3 Record Keeping

You're going to want to keep accurate records. There are many reasons for this, but the big reason is to have something to refer to. For example, it's very helpful to look through a past project's notes to see what tires you purchased, where and for how much. As you start to get a few Moneybikes completed it's nice to be able to look back and see what your average turnaround time has been, how much profit you typically make and so forth. I recommend doing, at a minimum, the following recordkeeping.

Receipts

Receipts document your expenses for each bike you flip. They are invaluable data to refer to in order to see how much you paid for various components and who you purchased them from. Save your receipts.

Sales Log

A sales log is a summary of the bikes you have flipped. It's a ledger that allows you to easily see the highlights of each bike you have flipped. A sales log shows you how much money you're making and how long it's taking you to completed bikes.

Columns you should consider having on your sales log include:

- Year, Make, Model of bike
- Cost of bike
- Total expenses (cost of bike plus additional costs)
- Sales price
- Profit (Sales price – total expenses)
- ROI
- Project Start Date

- Bike Listed Date
- Bike Sold Date

Transaction Paperwork

Always keep copies of bills of sale for each transaction (buying and selling) as well as any tax forms you needed. These are great to refer if need be. For each Moneybike you flip, you should have:

- A copy of the bill of sale for purchasing the bike
- A copy of the tax form (if applicable) for purchasing the bike
- A copy of the bill of sale for selling the bike
- A copy of the tax form (if applicable) for selling the bike

5.4 Knowledge Sources

You will need to be familiar with where to gain knowledge when you need it. There are four sources of knowledge that you need to be familiar with:

1. Maintenance Manuals
2. User Forums
3. Illustrated Parts Breakdown (IPB)
4. YouTube

Maintenance Manuals

Maintenance manuals are the bible for the bike. They are the ground truth. The good news is that they are readily available and can be purchased online. And here's the thing, you only have to buy the manual once. After that, every time you encounter that year and model of bike, you already have the manual for it. So, you only must pay the cost once.

Most bikes have well documented maintenance manuals. These manuals are either in digital or printed form. They have all the procedures spelled out, step by step, with all the details and plenty of pictures to guide you.

For metric bikes, Haynes is the company where you'll purchase your manuals. See the References Appendix for the website.[6]

For Harley-Davidson bikes, the company itself produces great manuals. Those are readily available in digital form on eBay.

You will need two other sources of knowledge in addition to the maintenance manual. The great news is that these other two sources of knowledge are free.

User Forums

Online user forums are a gold mine of knowledge. Each type of motorcycle has its own website filled with other riders who have deep knowledge of the bike, its design, and its maintenance. These websites are priceless when researching maintenance procedures and troubleshooting. Here is a list of my favorites:

- www.suzukisavage.com – This forum is hands-down, the best source of knowledge for the Suzuki LS650 Savage motorcycle. There is a tremendous amount of knowledge on how to troubleshoot issues as well as details on the recommended modifications to make the bike much more reliable.
- https://www.vulcanforums.com/ - Kawasaki Vulcan forum
- https://www.hondashadow.net/ - Honda Shadow forum
- https://www.volusiariders.com/ - Suzuki Boulevard / Volusia forum
- https://www.harley-davidsonforums.com/ - Harley-Davidson forum

There are other forums out there, but those are my go-to favorites. I've had a lot of success with the information found on these sites.

Illustrated Parts Breakdown

Everything manmade in our world is either a part or a fastener. Think about something like a dishwasher. It's a collection of parts, each with its own part number, all held together with nuts, bolts, and other fasteners (that also have their own part numbers).

Understand all the pieces and parts that make up a thing is important when trip to refurbish and flip the thing.

All the parts and fasteners for a motorcycle will be on a series of drawings. Those drawings show how everything *physically* fits together. Part "A" attaches to part "B" using a nut and bolt, etc., etc.

The collection of drawings for a bike is called its "Illustrated Parks Breakdown", or IPB for short. This is just a piece of the overall engineering for the bike. These drawings look something like this:

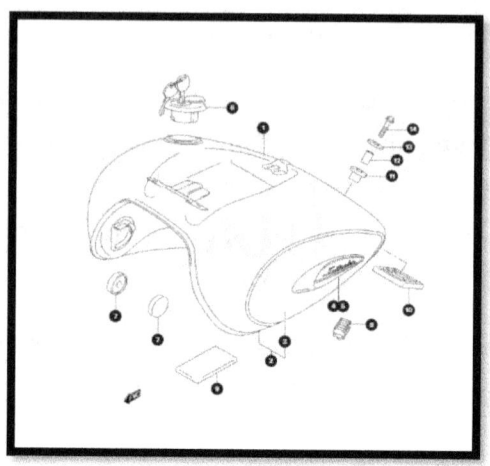

When you first look at a parts diagram, there's a lot there. It's like looking at a large, detailed map for the first time. You just get overloaded with visual information! Nothing makes sense! But, if you study the diagram for a few minutes, you will usually be able to start to make sense of what part fits where. Just like a large map—oh there's my town, my street, that lake down the road, etc. Parts diagrams are extremely useful in understanding what part goes where, what part you may be missing, and how things should be assembled.

YouTube

How in the world did we ever learn to do anything before YouTube? I'm a big fan of YouTube. The great thing about YouTube, for our purpose, is that we get to see someone else put the knowledge into practice. After reading through the maintenance manuals and user forums, we get to see somebody else attempt to do whatever it is that we're attempting. In doing so, we get to see firsthand the things that are hard, the stuff to look out for, special techniques that are handy, etc.

Putting the Knowledge Together

Maintenance manuals, user forums, illustrated parts breakdowns, YouTube—there's a lot of information out there. So, how do we put it all together?

Everything we do to refurbish our bike will be a part of a "task". Each task will require some prerequisite knowledge—some bit of know-how that we need to research first in order to accomplish the task. Here's what I generally do to learn how to accomplish a new task.

1. Check the maintenance manual. Is the task defined there? If so, read the procedure to get familiar.

2. If the task involves replacing or adding a part, review the illustrated parts diagram. Do I need more than the actual part I'm replacing? If so, add it to my basket to purchase. Does it make sense to replace some other part during the procedure? Ifo so, add it to the basket.
3. Check user forums. Have others attempted the task? If so, what lessons did they learn? Is there a pitfall that everyone seems to encounter? How did they overcome it?
4. Finally, search YouTube. Are there videos showing others accomplishing the task? Watch those and see what the task looks like.

The information is all out there. The trick is to be able to assemble the bits and pieces of information in a way that tells the story of how to accomplish the task.

Here's a real-life example. I was refurbishing a 2008 Suzuki Boulevard C50T. One of the tasks I had to accomplish was a valve job. I had adjusted valves on a riding lawn mower, but never a motorcycle. I knew the basic theory though—tighten or loosen a screw so that it meets some specification as measured by a feeler gauge.

I read through the maintenance manual. The basic procedure was to find top-dead-center on the engine (a specific point in the engines natural rotation), then remove the valve covers to access the screws, then make the adjustments. Simple! Not so fast.

In reading through the forums, I learned that there were many pitfalls and considerations with the procedure. If done incorrectly you can damage the engine beyond repair. Not good. First off, the engine must be completely cold—not been driven for at least 8 hours. People who attempt this procedure can very easily fail to find top-dead-center of the engine (as I did) resulting in valves that are too loose and chattery (as mine were). It is an extremely tight fit getting your hands in place to adjust the valves and you cannot see what you're doing. So, you must see with your fingers. When accessing the valves, there is a chance you can drop your tool into the core of the engine. That means the entire engine must come out and be disassembled to remove whatever you dropped—a task that was way beyond my skill at the time.

In watching YouTube, I found a video where a guy talks about these pitfalls and shows techniques on how to address them. To ensure you have top-dead-center he showed how to watch the valves in addition to the TDC mark. To adjust the valves, he showed how to make your own "tappet wrench" out of a simple Phillips head screw with an attached safety string. The string can be used to retrieve the little tool should you drop it in the engine. He also showed how to make the adjustments by feel and confirmed with a feeler gauge (a measuring device).

The maintenance manual gave me the procedure, the forums warned me of the pitfalls, and the forums plus YouTube showed the maintenance techniques to avoid the risky pitfalls. For that procedure, I was able to assemble the information into enough knowledge to get the job done. Full disclosure—it did take me two tries. But I'm very good at adjusting Suzuki engine valves now!

5.5 Parts Sources

You can purchase most parts needed online. Some suppliers only sell aftermarket parts (tires, batteries, etc.). Some suppliers sell aftermarket parts and OEM parts. Recommended suppliers are listed below:

- **J&P Cycles**[7] – great source for aftermarket parts such as tires, tubes, batteries, spark plugs, etc. Not an OEM vendor
- **Dennis Kirk** [8]– Another good source for aftermarket parts similar to J&P Cycles. Also not an OEM vendor.

- **RevZilla**[9] – Aftermarket and OEM parts. RevZilla has the best website for browsing OEM illustrated parts breakdowns. Their OEM parts tend to be on the expensive side though. RevZilla has some really good learning videos for basic motorcycle maintenance and repair as well. Be sure to check out their YouTube channel.
- **PartZilla**[10] – One of the lowest cost providers of OEM parts. Their illustrated parts breakdown website is good, but not quite as good as RevZilla.
- **Ron Ayers** [11]– The lowest prices OEM vendor, but they take the longest to ship. Their website is cumbersome as well. It's best to lookup your part number on another site's IPB, then search for it on this site.
- **Touchup Direct** [12]– A great source for touchup paint. The site allows you to search by year/model to find the color code of paint you need. Products tend to be on the expensive side but are high quality.
- **ColorRite**[13] – Another great source for touchup paint. ColorRite has been in business a long time and a great option for paint.

6 Case Studies

The following sections are real Moneybikes that I have completed. The numbers are real, the experiences are real and the profit I made was real. Hopefully, these case studies show how the Moneybike formula was put into practice, for real, to generate profit. These are all Suzuki bikes (my favorite), but the process works on any of the metric bike manufacturers discussed earlier. Notice that the sales price, profit, etc. do vary quite a bit from the basic Moneybike formula. The formula is the goal, but real life will have its variations and that's OK! Also notice, each bike was profitable—a testament to the Moneybike Formula!

6.1 2001 Suzuki Savage LS650

This was my very first Moneybike. It was both a Neglected Nelly and a Broken Betty. I had owned a Suzuki Savage before (The Angry Chui Wawa). So, I was pretty comfortable with working on this model of bike.

The bike had been sitting in someone's backyard, uncovered, for about a year. There was no muffler on the bike, and it wouldn't start. The seller had it listed for $700, and we negotiated a final price of $500. I knew this bike would require quite a bit to get it up to Moneybike standards.

If you look at the budget below, you'll notice I was $209.50 over budget on the Carb Rebuild line item. I had a hard time troubleshooting why this particular bike would not run right. I scoured the online user's forums, purchases several replacement parts for the carb, and eventually figured out what the issue was. Someone had used aftermarket components inside of the carburetor, not OEM parts. After purchasing the (much more expensive) OEM carb parts and installing them, the bike ran perfectly! Lesson learned—stick with OEM parts. Had I done that originally, I would have saved a few hundred bucks.

Item	Estimate	Actual	Delta
Initial Purchase			
Purchase Price	$ 500.00	$ 500.00	$ -
Sales Tax	$ 31.25	$ 49.00	$ 17.75
Inspection, Title and Registration	$ 85.00	$ 92.53	$ 7.53
Transportation Home	$ 100.00	$ 100.00	$ -
Parts & Restoration			
Tires ($15/ea to mount)	$ 200.00	$ 194.43	$ (5.57)
Carb Rebuild	$ 40.00	$ 249.50	$ 209.50
Fuel Cock	$ 25.00	$ 31.95	$ 6.95
Oil & filter	$ 20.00	$ 25.08	$ 5.08
Spark Plug(s)	$ 10.00	$ 3.38	$ (6.62)
Air Filter	$ 10.00	$ 18.35	$ 8.35
Seat covers	$ 60.00	$ 57.97	$ (2.03)
Muffler	$ 85.00	$ 79.00	$ (6.00)
Heat Shield	$ 20.00	$ 15.99	$ (4.01)
Touch-up Paint	$ 75.00	$ 47.45	$ (27.55)
Extras (Optional)			
Bike Cover	$ 30.00	$ 20.27	$ (9.73)
Windshield	$ 52.00	$ 102.97	$ 50.97
Saddlebags	$ 80.00	$ 129.17	$ 49.17
Handlebar grips	$ 35.00	$ 33.15	$ (1.85)
Mirrors	$ 25.00	$ 34.40	$ 9.40
Additional Parts	$ -	$ 107.67	$ 107.67
Sales Tax and Shipping	$ 50.00	$ 86.85	$ 36.85
Total Cost	$ 1,483.25	$ 1,979.11	$ 409.01
Sales Price	$ 2,600.00	$ 2,650.00	
Profit	$ 1,116.75	$ 670.89	
Margin	42.95%	25.32%	
ROI	75.29%	33.90%	

Also notice on this bike that I spent quite a bite on upgrades. This bike didn't have a muffler, so that was a given. But I also added a brand-new heat shield, new seat covers, windshield, saddlebags, handlebar grips and chrome mirrors.

When it was all said and done, all the extras were worth it. The bike was sold 2 days after being listed and it sold for my full asking price of $2,650. My total profit was $670.89, with an ROI of 33.9%.

6.2 2007 Suzuki Boulevard C50

This particular Suzuki Boulevard sported a custom blue flame paint job. It looked awesome. It also had upgraded "drag" handlebars with upgraded grips. It was a very sporty looking bike.

Every bike has a story. This bike's story was a sad one. The prior owner parked it in March of 2020 after contracting COVID-19. The bike, and the rider, never rode again. It was a Neglected Nelly for sure. The rider's son was selling the bike along with other assets from his father's estate. Very sad.

I bought the bike in 2022. It had been sitting for 2 years and all the fuel had evaporated from the tank, fuel lines, and fuel injectors. In refurbishing this bike, I learned all about how to restore a fuel system that has been sitting for some time. I replaced the fuel pump and learned how to setup my own fuel injector cleaning jig using a 9v battery (from YouTube). I learned how to clean rust from a gas tank using toilet bowl cleaner (hydrochloric acid) of all things.

The bike turned out great and sold for well above market value. I purchased the bike for $1,200 and my total cost was just over $2,600. The fuel pump and fuel sending unit (tell the odometer how much gas is left in the tank) were the most expensive components for this particular bike. This is when I discovered the Ron Ayers supplier and saved over $100 on parts. I made $2,543.41 in profit which was just about 100% ROI. On this bike, I doubled my money.

Item	Estimate	Actual	Delta
Initial Purchase			
Purchase Price	$ 1,200.00	$ 1,200.00	$ -
Online VIN Check	$ 11.00	$ 10.99	$ (0.01)
Sales Tax	$ 75.00	$ 113.00	$ 38.00
Inspection, Title and Registration	$ 100.00	$ 90.00	$ (10.00)
Transportation Home	$ 140.00	$ 140.00	$ -
Parts & Restoration			
Rear Tire, Tube, Rim Strip ($25 to mount)	$ 200.00	$ 159.89	$ (40.11)
Fuel Pump, O-Ring, Sending Unit	$ 700.00	$ 558.96	$ (141.04)
Gas tank cleanout	$ 30.00	$ 28.70	$ (1.30)
Injector cleaning	$ 50.00	$ 37.49	$ (12.51)
Oil change, K&N air filter clean, gear oil change	$ 40.00	$ 40.55	$ 0.55
Spark Plug(s)	$ 10.00	$ 5.78	$ (4.22)
Coolant	$ 15.00	$ -	$ -
Misc OEM bits	$ 85.00	$ 102.08	$ 17.08
Touchup Paint	$ 27.00	$ 26.39	$ (0.61)
Front Brake Pads	$ -	$ -	$ -
Rear Brake Drums	$ -	$ -	$ -
Extras (Optional)			
Bike Cover	$ 25.00	$ 25.61	$ 0.61
Windshield (MEM4120 w/ MEK1820 plates)	$ 80.00	$ -	$ -
Service Manual	$ 60.00	$ 64.00	$ 4.00
Suzuki Mode Select Switch	$ 16.95	$ 16.95	$ -
Suzuki Boulevard Keychain	$ 20.00	$ 10.54	$ (9.46)
Spare ignition key (37146-10F00)	$ 40.00	$ 25.66	$ (14.34)
Total Cost	$ 2,924.95	$ 2,656.59	$ (173.36)
Sales Price	$ 4,450.00	$ 5,200.00	
Profit	$ 1,525.05	$ 2,543.41	
Margin	34.27%	48.91%	
ROI	52.14%	95.74%	

6.3 2008 Suzuki Boulevard C50T

This bike was a Broken Betty. The prior owner reported that the bike didn't go over 50 mph and that the rear cylinder would not fire. Additionally, when you turned the bike on the fuel would leak down the side of the rear cylinder. So, it was basically a Molotov cocktail on wheels! Dangerous!

Other than that, it was a great bike though. It was in very good condition and had low miles for its age. In researching the online forums and inspecting the fuel injectors, I discovered that the incorrect O-Rings were used where the injectors are seated. This meant that they didn't for a tight seal and therefore leaked fuel when the bike turned on (and pressurized the fuel system). I didn't know how any of this stuff worked when I got the bike. But, by reviewing the maintenance manual and looking through the online forums I learned that:

- Fuel systems on fuel injected bikes are pressurized
- There are 2, different style of O-rings on a fuel injector
- Fuel injected bikes are way easier to troubleshoot and fix then carbureted bikes

After correcting the O-Ring issue, I also had to troubleshoot why the rear cylinder would not fire. What I discovered was that there was debris in the fuel rail. Most likely it was evaporated fuel that left the sticky, gummy residue. After cleaning that out with some compressed air, and putting the bike back together, it ran great! It was an awesome bike. Looking back, I probably could have negotiated the purchase price down a bit—$3,000 was a little high for this bike in the condition I found it. Regardless, it fetched a premium price when I was done with it, and I made a reasonable profit.

Item	Estimate	Actual	Delta
Initial Purchase			
Purchase Price	$ 3,000.00	$ 3,000.00	$ -
Online VIN Check	$ 11.00	$ 10.99	$ (0.01)
Tax, Title, Registration (SPV = 80% of $2335 = $1868 * 6.25%)	$ 210.00	$ 209.18	$ (0.82)
Transportation Home	$ 20.00	$ 18.39	$ (1.61)
Parts & Restoration			
Tires, Tubes, Rim Strips ($25 to mount/balance)	$ 380.00	$ 380.23	$ 0.23
Oil change, K&N air filter clean, gear oil change	$ 20.00	$ 22.36	$ 2.36
Spark Plug(s)	$ 10.00	$ 6.00	$ (4.00)
Coolant	$ -	$ -	$ -
Misc OEM bits	$ 80.00	$ 102.15	$ 22.15
Front Brake Pads	$ -	$ -	$ -
Rear Brake Drums	$ -	$ -	$ -
Extras (Optional)			
Bike Cover	$ 30.00	$ 28.81	$ (1.19)
Gas Tank Trim	$ 15.00	$ 10.13	$ (4.87)
Spare Ignition key	$ 25.00	$ 24.96	$ (0.04)
Fuel for test riding	$ 25.00	$ 15.05	$ (9.95)
CycleTrader Ad	$ -	$ 29.95	$ 29.95
Total Cost	$ 3,826.00	$ 3,858.20	$ 32.20
Sales Price	$ 5,400.00	$ 4,800.00	
Profit	$ 1,574.00	$ 941.80	
Margin	29.15%	19.62%	
ROI	41.14%	24.41%	

6.4 2005 Suzuki Boulevard C50

This two-town blue and black bike literally landed on my doorstep. I contacted the seller, and he was driving back from Colorado. He had driven to Colorado, from Texas, to purchase a bumper pull camper to flip. As it turned out, he was in the flipping business too. While in Colorado, he found this bike for sale at an estate sale. He bought it with the intention of wholesaling it to a flipper (like me). He altered his return route from Colorado, swung by my house, and dropped it off right in my driveway.

The bike was in good condition but very dirty. In fact, the bike only had 1,800 miles on it—it was basically brand new! It was a Neglected Nelly and wouldn't start. The previous owner was the original owner and rarely rode it. I ran the fuel injectors through my cleaning jig, added fresh gas, and the bike fired right up. After some cleaning and polishing, it was ready for sale and fetched a great profit.

Item	Estimate	Actual	Delta
Initial Purchase			
Purchase Price	$ 2,000.00	$ 2,000.00	$ -
Online VIN Check	$ 15.00	$ 14.95	$ (0.05)
Tax, Title, Registration	$ 215.00	$ 214.25	$ (0.75)
Transportation (Motorcycle Ramp)	$ 100.00	$ 96.84	$ (3.16)
Parts & Restoration			
Tires ($25/ea to mount and balance)	$ 350.00	$ 446.87	$ 96.87
Oil & Filter	$ 20.00	$ 49.10	$ 29.10
Spark Plug(s)	$ 6.00	$ 6.35	$ 0.35
Battery	$ 100.00	$ -	$ (100.00)
Fuel Pump	$ -	$ -	$ -
Coolant, Mystery Oil, Seafoam and other misc fluids	$ -	$ 15.00	$ 15.00
Misc OEM bits	$ 50.00	$ 66.99	$ 16.99
Front Brake Pads	$ -	$ -	$ -
Rear Brake Drums	$ -	$ -	$ -
Extras (Optional)			
Bike Cover	$ 30.00	$ 28.81	$ (1.19)
Keychains	$ 12.00	$ 11.73	$ (0.27)
Rear fender bib	$ 100.00	$ 47.80	$ (52.20)
Fuel for test riding	$ 25.00	$ 17.76	$ (7.24)
CycleTrader Ad	$ -	$ 29.95	$ 29.95
Total Cost	$ 3,023.00	$ 3,046.40	$ 23.40
Sales Price	$ 4,750.00	$ 4,600.00	
Profit	$ 1,727.00	$ 1,553.60	
Margin	36.36%	33.77%	
ROI	57.13%	51.00%	

I purchased the bike for $2,000 and put another $1,046 into it. It was listed for $4,600 for a profit of $1,553.60 which is 51% ROI.

7 Example Bill of Sale

Bill of Sale

I, We, _____ of _____ County, _____
            (Seller)   (State)

for and in consideration of _____ and other considerations to me and in
                                (Selling Price)

hand paid by _____ the receipt for which is hereby
                   (Purchaser)

acknowledged, have bargained, sold and delivered, and by these presents do sell

and delivery unto the said _____ in the County of _____,
                              (Purchaser)

the following vehicle:

_____

Year   Make   Model   VIN#

Seller	Purchaser
Printed Name: _____	Printed Name: _____
Address:	Address:
_____	_____
_____	_____
_____	_____
Signature: _____	Signature: _____

_____County, _____
                                 (State)

8 Example Spreadsheets

I'm one of those guys who puts everything in a Microsoft Excel spreadsheet. I love spreadsheets. They keep me organized and help me understand how my projects are going.

For Moneybikes, I have a single Excel workbook with six (6) tabs. I make a copy of this workbook for each Moneybike. Below are some screenshots and explanations of how I have created my spreadsheet.

SIX TABS:

Each of these tabs has a specific purpose. By keeping everything in one workbook, it makes it very easy to refer to later.

TAB 1: IN-PERSON INSPECTION

Check	Item	Comments
	Front tire - mfr date, tred depth	
	Front wheel - any obvious bending or malformities	
	Front brakes - check disk and caliper area for leaks, check pad depth, ops check front brakes	
	Forks - check trueness, check for leaky seals	
	Headlight - ops check	
	Front turn signals - ops check	
	Horn - ops check	
	Clutch - is it bent or marred? How does it feel?	
	Master Cylinder - check for leaks, fluid level	
	Rear view mirrors - anything damaged or missing?	
	Gas tank - dents?	
	Speedometer - dents, cracks, etc	
	Seats - any rips?	
	Rear blinkers - ops check	
	Rear brake like - ops check	
	Rear tire - mfr date, tred depth	
	Rear wheel - any obvious bending or malformities	
	Engine - visible damage? Anything missing?	
	Left foot controls (clutch) - anything missing?	
	Right foot controls (rear brake) - anything missing? Rear brake ops check	
	Exhaust headers and mufflers - anything missing or damaged?	
	Kick stand - present and functional?	
	VIN Check on Frame	
	Accessories (Windshield, bags, etc) - ops check and general condition	

I usually print out this sheet to take with me when traveling to conduct my In-Person Inspection. This is the inspection discussed previously in Section 4.3.

I usually make updates to this checklist after talking with the Seller and discussing the condition of the bike. During that discussion, there may be various things that I want to be sure to verify in person.

TAB 2: SPECS

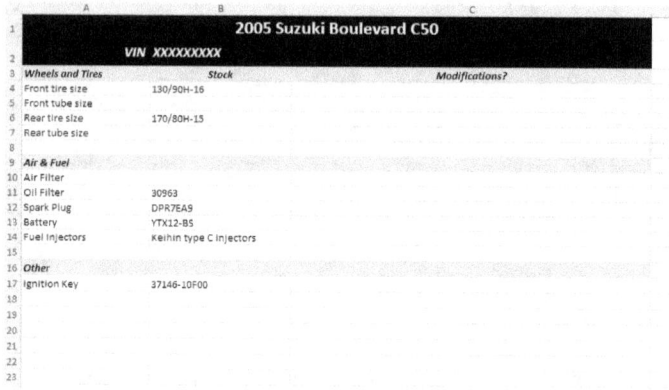

This tab is useful reference data. I found that I was continuously looking up specs over and over. So now, I look them up once and add them to this tab for convenience.

The specs I generally keep up with are shown in the picture. They're usually components of the motorcycle that I know will need replacing—tires, oil filter, etc.

TAB 3: PLAN

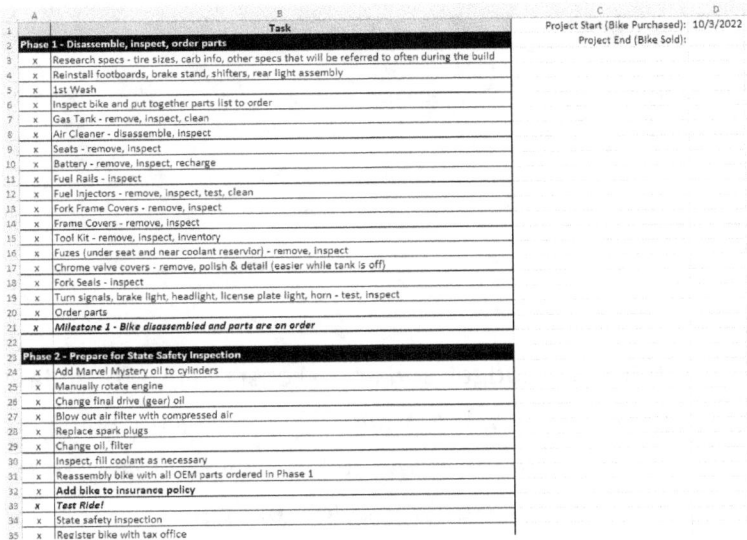

This tab has The Moneybike Gameplan. I review the gameplan for each bike to ensure it's applicable. It's rare that any 2 gameplans are exactly alike. They are very much bike dependent.

Also, I annotate the start and stop dates for the project. I consider the start date as the day I purchase the bike, and the stop date the day I sell it.

Tab 4: Budget

2007 Suzuki Boulevard C50				
Item	Estimate	Actual	Delta	Supplier
Initial Purchase				
Purchase Price	$ 1,200.00	$ 1,200.00	$ -	Facebook
Online VIN Check	$ 11.00	$ 10.99	$ (0.01)	ClearVIN
Sales Tax	$ 75.00	$ 111.00	$ [illegible]	Tax office
Inspection, Title and Registration	$ 100.00	$ 90.00	$ (10.00)	Tax office
Transportation Home	$ 140.00	$ 140.00	$ -	
Parts & Restoration				
Rear Tire, Tube, Rim Strip ($25 to mount)	$ 200.00	$ 150.89	$ (49.11)	Revzilla
Fuel Pump, O-Ring, Sending Unit	$ 700.00	$ 558.96	$ (141.04)	RonAyers.com
Gas tank cleanout	$ 30.00	$ 28.70	$ (1.30)	Brookshires
Injector cleaning	$ 50.00	$ 27.49	$ (22.51)	
Oil change, K&N air filter clean, gear oil change	$ 40.00	$ 40.55	$ 0.55	RonAyers.com
Spark Plug(s)	$ 10.00	$ 5.78	$ (4.22)	RonAyers.com
Coolant	$ 15.00	$ -	$ -	not needed
Misc OEM bits	$ 85.00	$ 102.08	$ 17.08	RonAyers.com
Touchup Paint	$ 27.00	$ 26.19	$ (0.81)	Color Rite
Front Brake Pads	$ -	$ -	$ -	not needed
Rear Brake Drums	$ -	$ -	$ -	not needed
Extras (Optional)				
Bike Cover	$ 25.00	$ 25.61	$ 0.61	Amazon
Windshield (MC[illegible] w/ [illegible] plates)	$ 80.00	$ -	$ -	not doing
Service Manual	$ 60.00	$ 64.00	$ 4.00	Haynes.com
Suzuki Mode Select Switch	$ 16.95	$ 16.95	$ -	RonAyers.com
Suzuki Boulevard Keychain	$ 20.00	$ 10.54	$ (9.46)	Giffords Hardware, Paris TX
Spare ignition key (37146-10F00)	$ 40.00	$ 25.66	$ (14.34)	Parts Suzuki (aftermarket Suzuki brand key)
Total Cost	$ 2,924.56	$ 2,656.59	$ (178.96)	
Sales Price	$ 4,400.00	$ 5,200.00		
Profit	$ 1,525.05	$ 2,543.41		
Margin	34.27%	48.91%		
ROI	52.14%	95.78%		

Purchases		
Date	Vendor	Amount
3/4/2022	Initial bike purchase	$ 1,200.00
3/4/2022	Transportation home	$ 140.00
3/6/2022	Brookshires - cleaner for tank rust	$ 28.70
3/4/2022	ClearVIN - vin check	$ 10.99
3/5/2022	Haynes Manual	$ 64.00
3/6/2022	RonAyers.com - gas tank parts and OEM bits	$ 686.44
3/8/2022	Revzilla - Rear tire and oil filter	$ 131.20
3/8/2022	Amazon - tube and rim strips	$ 28.33
3/8/2022	RonAyers.com - mode select switch	$ 16.95
3/8/2022	Amazon - Motorcycle Cover	$ 25.61
3/9/2022	Color Rite - touch up paint pen	$ 26.30
3/12/2022	Lowes - Rubber Stopper	$ 1.85
3/12/2022	Oreilly Auto Parts - K&N Recharge Kit, fuel line, hose clamps	$ 25.95
3/12/2022	Harbor Frieght - Alligator clips	$ 2.89
3/14/2022	RonAyers - refund for out of stock clamp	$ (19.62)
3/15/2022	Autozone - Gear oil, all purpose grease, fuel line for FI clean	$ 16.22
3/14/2022	Cash Savers - 9v battery for FI cleaning	$ 6.38
3/18/2022	Oreilly Auto Parts - Sealeam, oil change stuff	$ 36.33
3/24/2022	Tax Office - Tax, Title, Registration	$ 203.00
4/2/2022	Paris Suzuki - Mount tire ($25), extra key	$ 50.96
4/2/2022	Giffords Hardware	$ 11.54
	Total	$ 2,656.59

This tab has my budget and actual costs. I use formulas to keep track of how I'm progressing versus my plan. The red cells show items where I was over budget, and the green show where I was below budget.

It's OK to have some variation between what you originally planned and what actually happened. As you get a few bikes under your belt, you will get better at estimating. It's an art and take times.

I also keep a ledger on the right of the sheet showing all the purchases for the Moneybike. This is just another way to make sure I'm keeping costs under control.

TAB 5: PARTS LIST

Part Number	Description	Next Higher Assembly	Qty	Price (ea)	Total Price	Source	Comments
	IRC Motorcycle Tire Tube 130/90-16	Front Wheel	1	$20.30	$20.30	Amazon	
	IRC Rim Strips - 16"	Front Wheel	1	$6.15	$6.15	Amazon	
	IRC Motorcycle Tire Tube 170/80-15	Rear Wheel	1	$21.45	$21.45	Amazon	
	IRC Rim Strips - 15"	Rear Wheel	1	$6.05	$6.05	Amazon	
J&P Part #: 163-522	Shinko 777 Front Tire - Wide Whitewall	Front Wheel	1	$133.56	$133.56	J&P Cycles	
J&P Part #: 163-529	Shinko 777 Rear Tire - Wide Whitewall	Rear Wheel	1	$155.96	$155.96	J&P Cycles	
DPR7EA-9	NGK Standard Spark Plug		2	$3.99	$5.98	J&P Cycles	
HF138	Oil Filter, Hiflo		2	$8.99	$17.98	J&P Cycles	
2271190	Mustang Plain Fender Bib		1	$44.99	$44.99	J&P Cycles	
07120-0012B	BOLT	Fuel Pump	1	$2.72	$2.72	Partzilla	
09119-06001	BOLT,6X10	Battery Box	4	$10.12	$40.48	Partzilla	
09139-05025	SCREW 5X14	Odometer, Rear	1	$1.64	$1.64	Partzilla	
08139-05032	SCREW 5X18	Odometer, Front	2	$3.52	$7.04	Partzilla	
09329-10026	CUSHION	Gas Tank	1	$1.77	$1.77	Partzilla	
37146-10E00	KEY,BLANK (Suzuki) SZB-71	Wiring Harness	1	$20.71	$20.71	Partzilla	

In this sheet I document all the part numbers purchased for the bike. This is very useful reference information. I have found that I often refer to past projects to lookup what all I purchased, from where, and for how much.

This may seem like overkill but keeping track of what you are doing to the bike, all the way down to the part number, ensures that you're executing in a manner that is detail oriented. Remember, we're trying to create a finished product—something that could have just rolled out of the factory.

TAB 6: SELLING POINTS

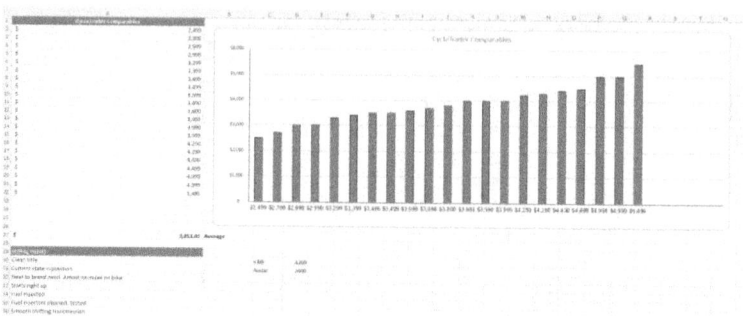

This tab is where I keep track of the bike's selling points during the project. I typically copy the list from the previous bike and then update it accordingly. Just like the plan and the budget, the list of selling points should be unique for each bike.

I also do a pricing analysis discussed previously in Section 4.6. This involves looking on CycleTrader for similar bikes of the same year, make and model. Then, write down all the list prices for any bike within some distance from you (100-mile radius makes sense for me). When you line all those prices up on a bar chart, you should price your bike on the high end. Remember, we're asking a premium price for our bike because it's a premium product.

9 References

1 https://www.bts.gov/content/automobile-profile

2 https://www.fortunebusinessinsights.com/motorcycle-market-105164

3 https://motorbikewriter.com/which-motorcycles-hold-value/

4 https://kbb.com/motorcycles

5 https://www.msf-usa.org/wp-content/uploads/2022/06/T-CLOCS_Inspection_Checklist.pdf

6 https://haynes.com/en-us/

7 https://www.jpcycles.com/

8 https://www.denniskirk.com/

9 https://www.revzilla.com/

10 https://www.partzilla.com/

11 https://www.ronayers.com/

12 https://touchupdirect.com/

13 https://www.colorrite.com/

www.ingramcontent.com/pod-product-compliance
Lightning Source LLC
Chambersburg PA
CBHW050246220526
45465CB00002B/569